T0011275

The Senate

by Daniel R. Faust

Consultant: John Coleman
Professor of Political Science, University of Minnesota
Minneapolis, Minnesota

BEARPORT
PUBLISHING

Minneapolis, Minnesota

Credits

Cover and Title Page, © Orhan Cam/Shutterstock; 3, © Dan Thornberg/Shutterstock; 4–5, © Orhan Cam/Shutterstock; 7, © mark reinstein/Shutterstock; 9, © Anna Moneymaker-Pool/Getty Images, © Scott J. Ferrell/Congressional Quarterly; 11, © ROBYN BECK/Getty Images; 13, © Win McNamee/Getty Images; 14, © Kevin Dietsch/Getty Images; 15, © Dan Thornberg/Shutterstock; 17, © Bettmann/Getty Images; 19, © Ryan Kelly/Getty Images; 21, © Chip Somodevilla/Getty Images, © Stefani Reynolds/Bloomberg/Getty Images, © Chip Somodevilla/Getty Images; 23, © Trong Nguyen/Shutterstock; 25, © Halfpoint/Shutterstock; 27, © Bill Clark/Getty Images; 28, © Orhan Cam/Shutterstock.

President: Jen Jenson
Director of Product Development: Spencer Brinker
Senior Editor: Allison Juda
Associate Editor: Charly Haley
Senior Designer: Colin O'Dea

Library of Congress Cataloging-in-Publication Data

Names: Faust, Daniel R., author.
Title: The Senate / by Daniel R. Faust.
Description: Minneapolis, Minnesota : Bearport Publishing Company, 2022. |
  Series: U.S. Government: need to know | Includes bibliographical references
  and index.
Identifiers: LCCN 2021023238 (print) | LCCN 2021023239 (ebook) | ISBN
  9781636916019 (library binding) | ISBN 9781636916088 (paperback) | ISBN
  9781636916156 (ebook)
Subjects: LCSH: United States. Congress. Senate—Juvenile literature. |
  Legislators—United States—Juvenile literature. | Legislation—United
  States—Juvenile literature.
Classification: LCC JK1276 .F38 2022 (print) | LCC JK1276 (ebook) | DDC
  328.73/071—dc23
LC record available at https://lccn.loc.gov/2021023238
LC ebook record available at https://lccn.loc.gov/2021023239

For more information, write to Bearport Publishing, 5357 Penn Avenue South, Minneapolis, MN 55419. Printed in the United States of America.

Contents

Where Do Laws Come From? 4

The Upper House. 6

Making the Laws of the Land 8

Working Together 12

More Powers 16

Keeping the Balance 18

Becoming a Senator. 20

Your Senators and You 24

Looking Forward 26

The Branches of Government 28

SilverTips for Success 29

Glossary 30

Read More .31

Learn More Online 31

Index 32

About the Author. 32

Where Do Laws Come From?

If you buy food, you can see the ingredients on the label. Why? It's the law. But where do laws come from? In the United States, laws are made by Congress. This is the **legislative** branch of the government. It includes the Senate.

The U.S. Congress is made up of the Senate and the House of Representatives. This body makes federal laws. Many other laws are made by state governments.

Congress meets in the
U.S. Capitol building.

The Upper House

When the founders wrote the Constitution, their first order of business was to create a legislative branch. Its power would be shared by two parts, called houses. The Senate is known as the upper house. Every state has 2 senators, for a total of 100 members.

Some founders wanted equal representation for each state in the legislative branch. Others wanted representation based on population. The Great Compromise of 1787 created two houses, each with their own form of representation.

Every once in a while, the Senate and the House of Representatives meet in what is called a joint session.

Making the Laws of the Land

Every law begins as a bill. A senator or other member of Congress writes this idea for a law. Then, the bill goes to a **committee** of other members. The committee researches and discusses the bill. If the committee agrees, it brings the bill to the full Senate.

There are many committees in the Senate. Each committee has a main focus, such as education, defense, or the environment.

Sometimes, senators ask experts to
answer a committee's questions.

The Senate debates the bill. Sometimes, they make changes. Once the bill is ready, the Senate votes. If enough senators vote yes, the bill goes to the House of Representatives. There, it goes through debating and voting again. If both houses agree on a bill, it is sent to the president.

The president can sign the bill to make it a law or veto it. A vetoed bill can still become a law if two-thirds of the members of each house vote to pass the bill anyway.

Senators often meet with the president and members of the House of Representatives to discuss bills.

Working Together

Why might senators disagree on a bill? Members of different **political parties** often have different views on issues such as taxes or health care. Senators usually vote in the same way as other members of their party.

The two largest political parties in the United States are the Democratic Party and the Republican Party. Members of the Senate who aren't in these two main parties are part of Third or Minor Parties.

Members from different parties need to work together to make laws.

The party with the most members in the Senate is called the majority party. The party with fewer members is called the minority party. Senators in both parties can have different roles in the Senate.

The vice president is also a part of the Senate. But they are not allowed to debate. The vice president votes only if there is a tie.

There are many extra jobs senators can have.

ROLE	RESPONSIBILITY
Majority Leader	Leads their party and decides what the Senate does each day
Minority Leader	Leads their party
Majority Whip	Helps the majority leader get votes from people in their party
Minority Whip	Helps the minority leader get votes from people in their party
Committee Chair	Leads a committee

More Powers

The Senate does more than just make laws. Along with the House of Representatives, the Senate has the power to approve the president's **budget**. They decide how the country's money will be spent. Both houses of Congress also share the power to declare war.

The Constitution gave the Senate even more powers. But some of them aren't as important today. In the past, the Senate voted on treaties with other countries. However, the president makes agreements outside of this system now.

The last time Congress declared war was in 1941. President Franklin D. Roosevelt asked them to do so.

Keeping the Balance

The Senate also has powers to balance the other branches of the federal government. The Senate **confirms** top members of the **judicial** and **executive** branches. The two houses of Congress also share the power to **impeach** some members of the other branches and put them on trial.

The system of checks and balances was important to the founders. They wanted to make sure no one branch of the government became too powerful.

The Senate questions would-be
members of the Supreme Court.

Becoming a Senator

Who can become a senator? In order to be elected, a person must be at least 30 years old. They have to be a U.S. citizen. And they must live in the state they want to represent.

Despite the age rule, a few senators have taken office before they turned 30. It turns out they didn't check birthdays in the early 1800s.

Most senators today are much older than 30.

Senators are elected by people from their state. They keep the job for terms that last six years. Every two years, some senators end their terms. They might try for reelection or leave the office. This means up to one-third of the Senate could change every other year.

Senators have no term limits. A person can be a senator for as long as they keep being elected.

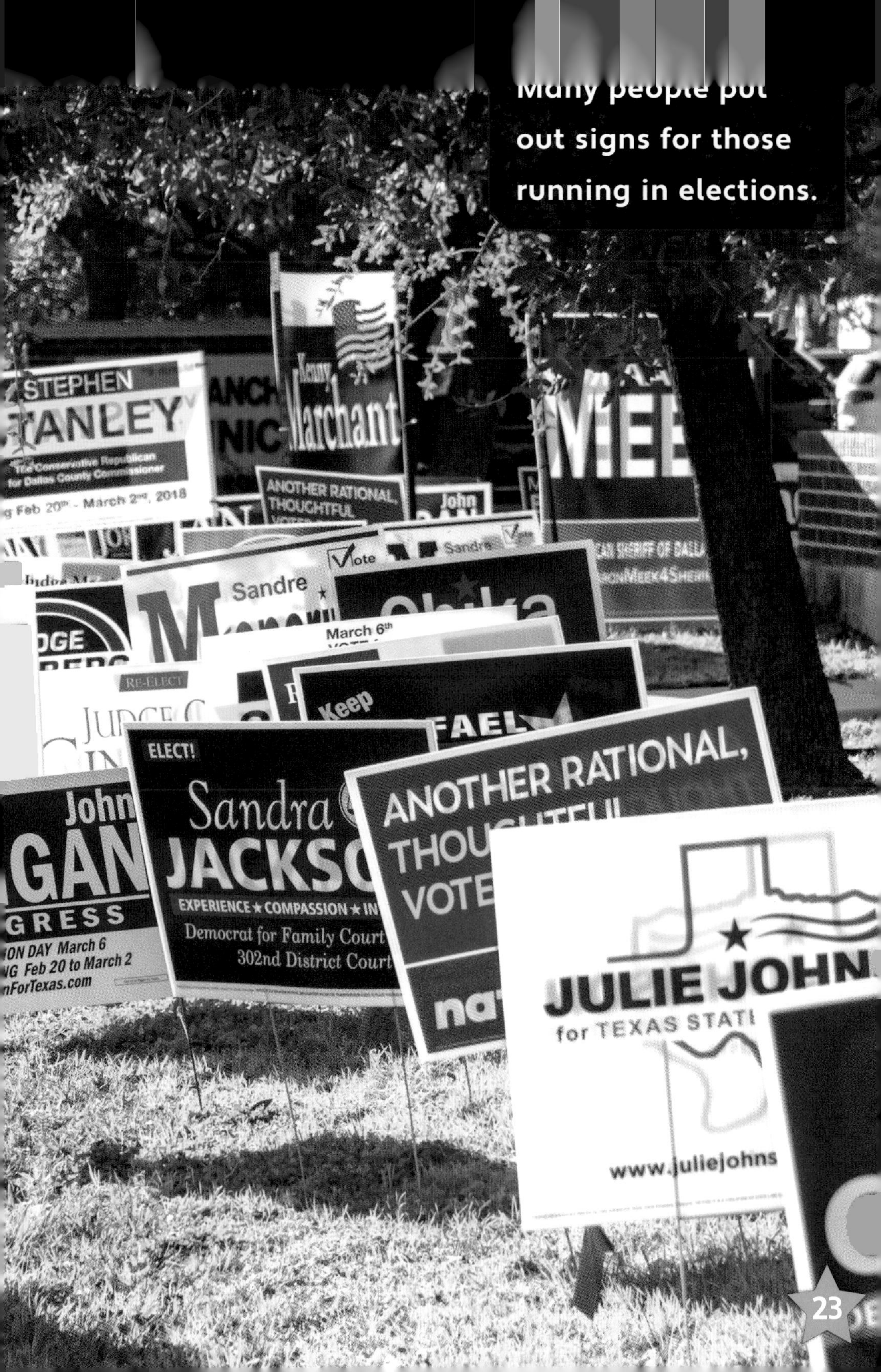

Many people put out signs for those running in elections.

Your Senators and You

A senator's job is to work for the people of their state. They are the peoples' voice in the government. Every voter and future voter has the right to have their voice heard. They can call, email, or post on social media.

Even if you are too young to vote, you can contact your senators to let them know what you think.

Protests can let senators know how people feel about issues.

Looking Forward

Today, the U.S. Senate has 100 members. Could that number change? Some people want Washington, D.C., and Puerto Rico to become states. If that happens, they will get their own senators. What does the future look like for the Senate? Only time will tell.

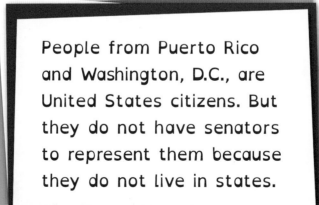

People from Puerto Rico and Washington, D.C., are United States citizens. But they do not have senators to represent them because they do not live in states.

Many people from Washington, D.C., want the district to be made a state.

The Branches of Government

Legislative Branch

Executive Branch

Judicial Branch

Makes laws
Made up of the Senate and the House of Representatives

Carries out laws
Made up of the president, the vice president, and the president's cabinet

Says if laws are followed correctly
Made up of the Supreme Court and other federal courts

The Senate

The Senate is a part of Congress. It has 100 members who work to make laws for the United States.

★ SilverTips for REVIEW

Review what you've learned. Use the text to help you.

Define key terms

bill

committee

federal government

legislative branch

representation

Check for understanding

What are the two houses in the legislative branch, and what are they called together?

Describe the steps needed for a bill to become a law.

Name one of the Senate's powers that is part of the checks and balances of government.

Think deeper

How does the Senate have an impact on your life? Name at least one example.

★ SilverTips on TEST-TAKING

★ **Make a study plan.** Ask your teacher what the test is going to cover. Then, set aside time to study a little bit every day.

★ **Read all the questions carefully.** Be sure you know what is being asked.

★ **Skip any questions** you don't know how to answer right away. Mark them and come back later if you have time.

Glossary

budget a plan to decide how money will be spent

committee a group of people who are chosen to make decisions about something

confirms gives approval to

constitution the system of laws for a country, state, or organization

executive related to the branch of a government that includes the president and vice president

federal having to do with the government of a nation

impeach to charge someone who holds public office with a crime

judicial related to the branch of government that includes courts and judges

legislative related to the branch of government with people who make laws

political parties groups of people with similar values that join together to make things happen in the government

representation doing something for another person or group; representatives are the people who act for others

veto the power of a person to decide that something will not be approved

Read More

Alexander, Vincent. *Legislative Branch (My Government).* Minneapolis: Jump! 2019.

McDaniel, Melissa. *The U.S. Congress (A True Book: Why It Matters).* New York: Children's Press, 2020.

Smith-Llera, Danielle. *Exploring the Legislative Branch (Searchlight Books: Getting into Government).* Minneapolis: Lerner Publications, 2020.

Learn More Online

1. Go to **www.factsurfer.com** or scan the QR code below.

2. Enter "**The Senate**" into the search box.

3. Click on the cover of this book to see a list of websites.

Index

bill 8, 10–12

budget 16

checks and balances 18

committee 8–9, 15

Congress 4–5, 8, 16–18, 26, 28

debate 10, 14

election 20, 22–23

House of Representatives, the 4, 7, 10–11, 16, 28

impeach 18

judicial branch 18, 28

laws 4, 8, 10, 13, 16, 28

legislative branch 4, 6, 28

majority 14–15

minority 12, 14–15

president 10–11, 14, 16–17, 28

About the Author

Daniel R. Faust is a freelance writer of fiction and non-fiction. He lives in Brooklyn, NY.